# Table of Contents

# AUTHOR'S INTRODUCTION

Dear Educator:

Teachers have always used a variety of assessment strategies to help them evaluate children's progress and to make instructional decisions. Taken together, these strategies can form a coherent assessment system.

A good assessment system has three essential elements. First, it includes a variety of informal and formal assessments. Second, it helps teachers integrate assessment during instruction and use that information to adjust their teaching. Finally, a good assessment system includes both teacher and child self-assessment throughout the learning process.

*Houghton Mifflin Reading* provides teachers with assessment options to fill all these needs. In this program you will find Integrated Theme Tests, Theme Skills Tests, Benchmark Progress Tests, and the new Leveled Reading Passages. In this test booklet you will find the *Teacher's Annotated Edition* of the Integrated Theme Tests and the corresponding Alternative Format Tests for each theme.

*Houghton Mifflin Reading* also provides extensive support for assessment integrated into the instructional plan in the *Teacher's Edition* that accompanies the Anthology. There you will find informal diagnostic checks and suggestions for reteaching, student self-assessments, comprehension and fluency checks, and test-taking strategies. The *Teacher's Assessment Handbook* provides other assessment strategies and information on using the results of assessment to plan instruction.

Not all teachers, children, or school districts need the same assessment system. By reviewing the various options in *Houghton Mifflin Reading*, you can determine which pieces best meet your needs. Enjoy the many opportunities assessment provides to get to know your students and to help them grow.

*Sheila Valencia*

# FEATURES AT A GLANCE

## Integrated Theme Tests

✔ Apply theme skills to new authentic reading material.

✔ Include both narrative and expository text.

✔ Have a short selection that complements the main selection so that students can compare texts.

✔ Provide theme-related reading and writing tasks.

✔ Test in a format that reflects instruction.

✔ Integrate reading strategies, comprehension, word skills, writing, and language.

✔ Include written and multiple-choice answers.

✔ Can be used as performance assessment.

✔ Are easy to administer.

✔ Can be adapted to meet individual needs.

✔ Have an easy-to-use *Teacher's Annotated Edition* with rubrics and sample answers at point of use.

# USING THE INTEGRATED THEME TESTS

## PURPOSE AND DESCRIPTION

### Purpose

The Integrated Theme Tests evaluate students' progress as readers and writers in a format that reflects instruction. By providing an opportunity to apply skills to theme-related text selections, each Integrated Theme Test is an indicator of how well students have learned and are able to apply the skills and strategies developed in the theme.

### Description

The Integrated Theme Tests include authentic reading selections and writing prompts that relate to the corresponding themes in the Anthology. Each test provides a main selection and a short related piece for the purpose of comparing texts. Students are asked to respond to the selections in four parts: Reading Strategy, Comprehension/Comparing Texts, Structural Analysis and Vocabulary, and Writing and Language. In addition, there are optional sections for Listening Comprehension and Self-Assessment.

- **Reading Strategy:** While the best time to incorporate reading strategies is during classroom instruction, strategies are included in the test as a model of good reading practice and to help teachers evaluate how well students use them. The reading strategy questions are carefully placed within each selection depending on the text and the strategy.

- **Comprehension/Comparing Texts:** This section includes both written and multiple-choice questions. There are two sets of questions. The first set of questions follows the main selection and evaluates the student's ability to comprehend and apply theme skills to the authentic reading passage. The second set of questions follows the second selection and focuses on the student's ability to comprehend and compare texts.

- **Structural Analysis and Vocabulary:** This part consists of multiple-choice questions that assess the student's ability to apply structural analysis and vocabulary skills taught in the theme to words related to the test selection.

- **Writing and Language:** This part assesses a student's writing fluency and ability to apply writing skills to a particular writing mode taught in the Reading-Writing Workshop. Students are given a prompt, suggestions for planning their writing, and guidelines. A proofreading exercise and two additional writing skills questions are also included.

- **Listening Comprehension (optional):** This optional section includes a short teacher read-aloud selection followed by one written and two multiple-choice questions to test the student's ability to comprehend material that is read aloud.

- **Self-Assessment (optional):** Concluding each Integrated Theme Test is an optional Self-Assessment survey. By completing this self-evaluation survey, students provide information about their reading attitudes and habits and about their own perception of their growth as readers.

# ADMINISTERING THE INTEGRATED THEME TESTS

Administer each Integrated Theme Test after students have completed the corresponding theme in the Anthology.

## Grouping

The Integrated Theme Tests are designed to be group administered, with students reading and responding individually at their own pace. However, you may administer the test to small groups or individual students in order to provide extra support.

## Pacing

Most students will be able to complete each test in about one hour. Allow enough time for students to finish the test without rushing. Many teachers prefer to give the test in two sittings of 30–40 minutes on successive days as follows:

- Day 1: Reading Strategy, Comprehension/ Comparing Texts, Structural Analysis and Vocabulary
- Day 2: Writing and Language, Listening Comprehension (optional), Self- Assessment (optional)

## Introducing the Test (Day 1)

- Read aloud the introduction that precedes the test selection.
- Explain that you expect students to complete Parts 1, 2, and 3.
- Assure students that they can look back at the text to help them answer the questions.
- You may want to have students stop after they have completed each part of the test so you can read aloud and explain the directions for the next part to the whole class.
- Emphasize that you are interested in how well students understand the selection. Explain that they should do their best work but do not have to display perfect spelling and grammar.
- Point out that the multiple-choice questions have only one correct answer.

## Introducing the Test (Day 2)

- Point out that in the second section of the test students will write a response in the style of the writing mode they studied in the Reading-Writing Workshop. They will also proofread a selection for errors and answer two multiple-choice questions.
- Read aloud the writing prompt and directions. Feel free to have a short discussion with students to help them think about topics for writing. Explain to students that their planning will not be graded.
- You may choose to have students do first-draft writing or revise their writing as part of the test. Explain what you expect of their first draft or of their revised draft.
- If you administer Listening Comprehension, explain that you will read aloud a selection once and then read questions for students to answer.
- Tell students that while they will not be scored on the Self-Assessment survey, they should complete it to help them think about what they have learned.

# REACHING ALL LEARNERS

By varying the amount of support you provide, you can adapt the Integrated Theme Tests to meet individual students' needs.

## Working Independently

Most students will be able to complete the tests independently. They will do their best work if the test is given in a comfortable and supportive manner. The following steps will help establish this atmosphere:

- Read the test introduction aloud, addressing any questions before the students begin.

- During the test, circulate among the students to make sure they understand the instructions.

- Allow students time to finish the test without rushing.

## Partial Support

For students who need a limited amount of support, use some or all of the following suggestions:

- Before students read the test selection, use the Prior Knowledge/Building Background and Purpose for Reading activities on the Providing Support page, which is in the *Teacher's Annotated Edition* of each test.

- Allow students to read the selection independently or cooperatively with a partner.

- Coach students if they need help understanding questions or formulating their answers.

## Full Support

For students who need more support, use the following suggestions:

- Use the Prior Knowledge/Building Background activity and the Purpose for Reading activity.

- Have students read the selection in segments, using the Supported Reading suggestions on the Providing Support page. Encourage students to then answer the questions orally in the Supported Reading group, emphasizing the reasons for their answers.

- If some students need further support, have them work individually with you to answer the test questions orally.

## Alternative Format Tests

Even with the support suggested above, an occasional student may still have difficulty accessing test selections. In this case, you may wish to use the Alternative Format of the Integrated Theme Tests. The Alternative Format Tests are a good choice for students who normally use the *Leveled Readers* selections in class.

The Alternative Format Tests include a summary of the main test selection, written at a lower reading level, plus comprehension questions to be answered either orally or in writing. The Alternative Format Tests can be administered individually or in a small group. They are provided as blackline masters in the back of this *Teacher's Annotated Edition.*

# GUIDELINES FOR SCORING

## Written-Response Questions (Scoring Using a Rubric)

A scoring rubric has been specifically designed for each open-ended question in the Integrated Theme Tests. Each rubric contains sample answers, the score given for the answer, and the criterion used in determining this score. Because student approaches to each question will vary, use your own interpretation of the response to help you determine scores for answers that are different from the sample answers. You should focus on the content and not be distracted by mechanics, spelling, or handwriting. Give a score of 0, 1, 2, 3, or 4. Scoring rubrics may occasionally contain only two sample answers, with scores of 2 and 4. For these questions, you may also assign a score of 1 or 3 if you feel a student's answer merits it.

## Multiple-Choice Questions

Students should fill in the circle next to the correct answer and leave the other circles blank. Use the scoring formula at the bottom of the test page to determine the score for the number of correct answers.

## Writing Skills

In evaluating student writing responses, the most emphasis should be given to ideas, organization, and effective communication. Usage and mechanics are also important, but should be given less emphasis. Use the scoring rubric and sample answers in the same manner as in scoring written comprehension questions.

## Proofreading

The proofreading activity requires students to correct the grammar and spelling errors in the text given. Use the scoring formula at the bottom of the test page to determine the score for the number of correct answers.

## Listening Comprehension (optional)

Because this test is optional, a scoring formula is not included. If you choose to administer the test, evaluate students on the strengths and weaknesses of their responses to the read-aloud selection.

## Self-Assessment (optional)

While there are no right or wrong answers to the questions in the Self-Assessment survey, students' responses can help you to determine how their reading attitudes may affect their comprehension and performance on the Integrated Theme Tests. Response to the survey can best be evaluated by considering the following questions:

- Does the student express clear opinions about what he or she has read? Do these opinions accurately reflect his or her attitudes about reading, based on what you already know?

- What attitude does the student express for this particular theme? How might this have affected the student's performance on this test?

# USING TEST RESULTS TO PLAN FOR INSTRUCTION

## DEVELOPING AND INTERPRETING STUDENT PROFILES

### Recording Part Scores

There are score lines provided throughout the Integrated Theme Tests to help you calculate students' scores for various test parts. Occasionally, a score must be multiplied by a given number. Transfer each part total onto the Test Record as shown below. Then calculate the total score.

### Developing Student Profiles

Develop the overall Student Profile on the Integrated Theme Test Record by drawing a line connecting the scores for each part.

You may wish to plan individual or small group conferences to discuss the test selection and questions with students who exhibited similar difficulties on the test. Review the test items, clarifying and discussing answers. Information gathered in these conferences will help you determine if the student's score is due to poor comprehension, a misunderstanding of directions, or other factors. This will help you evaluate each student's overall test performance more completely.

### Interpreting Student Profiles

Look for patterns in the Student Profile that identify specific skill strengths and weaknesses. Use the Integrated Theme Test results in combination with information from other assessments, classroom observations, and other student work to make decisions about students' progress and needs. Once you have determined the students who need extra support or a challenge, you can plan appropriate skill review or instruction for the next theme.

If a student has overall poor test scores but does not seem to be struggling in class, check whether time allotment, directions, or test format may be contributing factors. Also consider the level of support a student is receiving in class. An independent task such as this test may disclose that the student is relying on classroom support for reading comprehension. The *Teacher's Assessment Handbook* has other assessment options to help you analyze students' understanding of the skills.

Overall poor performance on tests and in class may indicate that the assigned work is too difficult. You may wish to have the student use the *Leveled Readers,* audios, and selection summaries during the next theme.

# PLANNING FUTURE INSTRUCTION

Here are some suggestions for using information obtained from the test to plan instruction for individual needs.

## Extra Support

- If a student has difficulty with comprehension, be sure to give the student sufficient time to reread the selection. You might guide students through the reading if they have demonstrated significant difficulty. If a student is able to clarify his or her errors and demonstrate understanding of the questions missed, move on. If not, you may want to use the appropriate Reteaching lessons and Skill Trace in the *Teacher's Edition* to make sure the student is prepared for the next time the skill will be addressed.

- If a student needs additional help in general comprehension, you might help her or him build understanding of the just-completed theme through discussion and explanation, individually or in small groups. For reading selections in future themes, the student may need more extensive building of background knowledge and vocabulary. The student may also benefit from cooperative or teacher-supported reading.

- If a student has difficulty with structural analysis and vocabulary, she or he may need individual or small-group instruction in decoding skills. The student may also benefit from reading and rereading of easier materials, such as the *Leveled Readers* selections. In working on future themes, the student may benefit from teacher-directed reading or cooperative reading with students who have advanced decoding skills.

- If a student demonstrates difficulty in writing, you may provide more practice and support with writing. You might allow more time for writing and review Writing Traits lessons as needed. Use the students' Integrated Theme Tests to help them self-evaluate their writing. Discuss qualities of good writing and help them set goals for future writing.

## Challenge

- If a student shows advanced comprehension, use suggestions in the Challenge boxes when reading the next selection, and assign him or her additional challenging reading material from the *Leveled Readers* or the *Houghton Mifflin Classroom Bookshelf*.

- If a student shows advanced ability in structural analysis and vocabulary, assign Challenge/Extension activities for the skill in the Resources section of the *Teacher's Edition*.

- If a student demonstrates superior writing ability, you may assign her or him Challenge writing activities in the Resources section of the *Teacher's Book*.

## Additional Support Materials

See pages T10–T11 of this *Teacher's Annotated Edition* for more resources provided by *Houghton Mifflin Reading* to help you plan appropriate instructional support.

# HOUGHTON MIFFLIN READING
## RESOURCES FOR REACHING ALL LEARNERS

If test results indicate that a student needs extra support or challenge in certain skill areas, you may consider modifying instruction in the next theme by using the following resources in *Houghton Mifflin Reading*.

| | Extra Support/Intervention | Challenge |
|---|---|---|
| **Part 1: Reading Strategy** | • *Teacher's Edition,* Back to School: Strategy Workshop<br>• *Teacher's Edition:* Strategy Review, Strategy/Skill Modeling, Strategy Focus, Extra Support/Intervention Strategy Modeling boxes<br>• *Practice Book:* Strategy Poster | • Other Reading: Theme Paperbacks (above level books), Classroom Bookshelf (above level books), Leveled Readers (above level) |
| **Part 2: Comprehension/ Comparing Texts** | • *Teacher's Edition,* throughout each selection: Building Background, Introducing Vocabulary, Extra Support/Intervention and Previewing the Text boxes, Guiding Comprehension questions, Reading for Understanding, Wrapping Up<br>• *Teacher's Edition,* Resources: Reteaching Lessons for Comprehension Skills<br>• Leveled Readers<br>• Other Reading: Theme Paperbacks (below level), Classroom Bookshelf (below level) | • *Teacher's Edition,* throughout each selection: Challenge boxes, Assignment Cards, Responding questions and activities<br>• *Teacher's Edition,* Resources: Challenge/Extension Activities for Comprehension<br>• Other Reading: Theme Paperbacks (above level books), Classroom Bookshelf (above level), Leveled Readers (above level) |

# RESOURCES FOR REACHING ALL LEARNERS (continued)

|  | Extra Support/Intervention | Challenge |
|---|---|---|
| **Part 3: Structural Analysis and Vocabulary** | • *Teacher's Edition,* Back to School: Phonics/Decoding Lesson in the Strategy Workshop<br>• *Teacher's Edition,* throughout each selection: Developing Key Vocabulary, Vocabulary boxes<br>• *Teacher's Edition,* Resources: Reteaching Lessons for Structural Analysis Skills<br>• CD-ROM: Lexia Quick Phonics Assessment | • *Teacher's Edition,* Vocabulary Skills lesson: Expanding Your Vocabulary<br>• *Teacher's Edition,* Resources: Challenge/Extension Activities for Vocabulary<br>• CD-ROM: Wacky Web Tales |
| **Part 4: Writing and Language** | • *Teacher's Edition,* Reading-Writing Workshop: Student Writing Sample, Tips for Getting Started, Tips for Organizing, Writing Traits, Student Self-Assessment<br>• *Teacher's Edition,* Resources: Reteaching Lessons for Grammar Skills<br>• *Teacher's Edition,* Spelling: Basic Words, Extra Support/Intervention box<br>• *Practice Book,* Writing Traits | • *Teacher's Edition,* Reading-Writing Workshop: Reading as a Writer, Publishing and Evaluating<br>• *Teacher's Edition,* throughout each selection: Journal Writing, Genre Lessons, Writer's Craft Lessons<br>• *Teacher's Edition,* Resources: Writing Activities<br>• *Teacher's Edition,* Spelling: Challenge Words, Challenge box<br>• CD-ROM: Wacky Web Tales |
| **Part 5: Listening Comprehension (optional)** | • *Teacher's Edition:* Teacher Read Aloud, Listening/ Speaking/Viewing | • *Teacher's Edition:* Listening/ Speaking/Viewing |

For more extra support and challenge ideas, consult the *Extra Support Handbook* and the *Challenge Handbook.*

# Off to Adventure!

## Level 3, Theme 1

## Integrated Theme Test Record

Student _____   Date _____

**Student Profile**

| Part | Part Scores: | Excellent Progress | Good Progress | Some Progress | Needs Improvement |
|---|---|---|---|---|---|
| **1: Reading Strategy**<br>• predict/infer | Items 1–2 | 7–8 | 5–6 | 3–4 | 0–2 |
| **2: Comprehension/Comparing Texts**<br>• sequence of events, making inferences, cause and effect | Items 3–4, 10 (written) | 10–12 | 7–9 | 4–6 | 0–3 |
| | Items 5–9, 11–13 (multiple-choice) | 21–24 | 12–18 | 6–9 | 0–3 |
| **3: Structural Analysis and Vocabulary**<br>• base words, syllabication, inflected endings -ed and -ing<br>• multiple-meaning words | Items 14–18 | 12–15 | 9 | 6 | 0–3 |
| **4: Writing and Language**<br>Writing Fluency: Personal Narrative<br>Proofreading<br>• short vowels: a, e, i, o, u; vowel-consonant-e<br>• what is a sentence?, kinds of sentences, subjects and predicates<br>Writing Skills<br>• using commas in dates and places<br>• capitalizing days and months | Item 19 Fluency | 24 | 18 | 12 | 0–6 |
| | Item 20 Language | 10–12 | 6–8 | 4 | 0–2 |
| | Items 21–22 Writing Skills | 6 | | 3 | 0 |
| **5: Listening Comprehension (optional)**<br>• making inferences, cause and effect | | Since the Listening Comprehension subtest is optional, it is not included in the total score. If you choose to give the subtest, evaluate answers for evidence of strengths and weaknesses. | | | |
| **6: Self-Assessment (optional)**<br>• self-assessment/reflection<br>• developing preferences | Poster | Scoring of Self-Assessment is not recommended. Evaluate answers for evidence of metacognitive growth. | | | |

**Total Score:** _____ /100

Test taken independently ☐
Test taken with partial support ☐
Test taken with full support ☐

Additional Comments _____

_____

_____

# PROVIDING SUPPORT

Most students should be able to take the test independently. For those needing more support, use the following suggestions.

## Partial Support

- Use one or both of these activities before students read:

---

**Prior Knowledge/Building Background**

Use the following ideas to spark discussion about the selection:
- Ask students whom they would name as someone who has adventures.
- Ask students to explain what they think an adventure is.

---

**Purpose for Reading**

Have students read to find out what kind of adventures Amelia Earhart had.

---

- Allow students to read the selection cooperatively with a partner.
- Help students understand the questions and plan their answers.

## Full Support

- Use **Prior Knowledge/Building Background** and **Purpose for Reading** activities above.
- **Supported Reading** Have students read the selection in segments. After each segment, use the questions to support students' reading:

---

**Supported Reading**

Segment 1: From the beginning to the end of page 5
   Question: *Why did Amelia want to fly planes?*
Segment 2: From the beginning of page 6 to the end of the selection
   Question: *Why might some people think Amelia Earhart is a hero?*

---

- Encourage students to answer the test questions independently. If necessary, have them answer the questions orally in a group.
- For further support, have students work individually with you to answer the questions orally.

Name _____

# Off to Adventure!

In Off to Adventure! you read stories about exciting and unusual adventures. Now you will read the true-life story of a young woman who dreamed of flying, and how she worked to make this dream come true.

There are questions to answer before, during, and after your reading. You may go back to the selection to help you answer the questions.

## 1 READING STRATEGY

1. **Predict/Infer** Look at the title and pictures for this story. What do you think you will learn about Amelia Earhart from reading this story?

| Score | 0 | 1 | 2 | 3 | 4 |
|---|---|---|---|---|---|
| Criterion | Illegible or no answer | Makes a vague prediction | Makes an obvious prediction or states given fact | Makes a plausible prediction, but it needs to be focused on character | Makes a prediction that considers the story's title and its illustrations |
| Sample Answer | | *I think I will learn what she did.* | *I will learn that she was a pilot.* | *I will learn about trips she took in planes.* | *I will learn how her dream of flying became real.* |

# Young Amelia Earhart:
## A Dream to Fly

**by Susan Alcott**

Amelia Earhart was America's greatest woman pilot. Her daring adventures made her famous all over the world.

Amelia was born in Kansas in 1897. In those days, girls had to act like ladies. They could not play games as boys did. But Amelia and her younger sister Muriel were lucky. Their mother and father believed girls and boys should be treated the same.

Amelia and Muriel were allowed to play baseball, football, and other sports. Amelia loved to think of exciting games to play.

One winter day Amelia, Muriel, and their friends went sledding. But just as Amelia was zooming down a big hill, a large, horse-drawn wagon crossed the street in front of her.

The driver did not see Amelia. And there was no time for Amelia to stop. But Amelia was calm. She steered the sled *underneath* the horse!

Amelia saw her first airplane at the Iowa State Fair when she was 11 years old. She did not know then that one day airplanes would change her life.

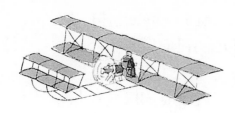

When Amelia grew up, she worked as a nurse. One day Amelia and a friend saw some pilots doing tricks in the air. As she watched the planes turn and dive, Amelia got very excited.

"I must learn to fly," Amelia said. And so she began taking lessons.

Amelia learned everything about planes. She could even take an engine apart and put it back together!

Amelia learned how to fly in all kinds of weather. Her teacher taught her to fly at night, too.

Finally, after practicing for a long time, Amelia got her pilot's license. She was 25 years old.

**Stop here and answer Question 2.
Then continue reading.**

---

## READING STRATEGY (continued)

2. **Predict/Infer** Based on what you have read about Amelia Earhart, what do you think she will do now that she has her pilot's license?

| Score | 0 | 1 | 2 | 3 | 4 |
|---|---|---|---|---|---|
| Criterion | Illegible or no answer | Makes a vague prediction | Makes an obvious prediction or states given fact | Makes a reasonable but general prediction | Makes a prediction consistent with story information |
| Sample Answer | | *I think she will learn to do something else.* | *I think she will fly a plane.* | *I think she will take a trip in a plane.* | *I think she will have many adventures in her plane.* |

Rubric Score for Items 1–2 (x 1) _____
8

Soon Amelia became the greatest woman pilot in the world.

In 1932, Amelia flew across the Atlantic Ocean by herself. No woman had ever done that.

Amelia set many records in her little plane. People all over the world cheered her on.

In 1937, Amelia decided to do something no one had ever done before. She wanted to fly around the world. She and a man named Fred Noonan began their around-the-world adventure in Miami, Florida.

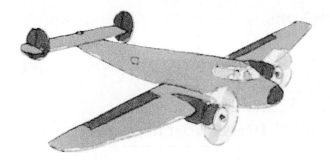

For a month, everything went well. Then Amelia and Fred headed for Howland Island in the Pacific Ocean.

But something went wrong. Amelia and Fred never arrived at Howland Island. And no one ever heard from them again.

No one knows what happened to Amelia Earhart. Most people think her plane crashed in the ocean.

But Amelia has never been forgotten. Her brave spirit and exciting adventures still inspire people today.

## 2 COMPREHENSION

**Write your answers to these questions.**

3. Look at the chart below.  What is one more reason why Amelia Earhart learned to fly? *(cause and effect)*

| Cause (Why does it happen?) | Effect (What happens?) |
|---|---|
| 1. She enjoyed doing exciting activities while growing up.<br><br>2. *She got excited watching planes do tricks.* <br><br> _____ | Amelia Earhart learned to fly. |

| Score | 0 | 2 | 4 |
|---|---|---|---|
| Criterion | Illegible or no answer | Identifies a cause that is vague or partially correct | Identifies the correct cause |
| Sample Answer | | *She watched planes.* | *She got excited watching planes do tricks.* |

4. Why did Amelia Earhart want to fly around the world? *(making inferences)*

| Score | 0 | 1 | 2 | 3 | 4 |
|---|---|---|---|---|---|
| Criterion | Illegible or no answer | Gives a very general response | Gives an answer that is true, though not connected to character | Gives a simple inference consistent with story information | Gives an inference that shows understanding of the character |
| Sample Answer | | *She loved to fly.* | *No one had ever done it before.* | *She wanted to be the first one to do it.* | *She enjoyed adventure and liked taking chances.* |

Rubric Score for Items 3–4 (x 1) _____
8

*In considering a student's score for Question 3, also feel free to give a score of 1 or 3, between those indicated above.*

**Read each question and fill in the circle next to the best answer.**

5. According to the story, when did Amelia Earhart get her pilot's license? *(sequence of events)*

   ● **A.** at the age of 25

   ○ **B.** in 1932

   ○ **C.** in 1937

   ○ **D.** when she first saw an airplane

6. Which of these events happened after Amelia Earhart got her pilot's license? *(sequence of events)*

   ○ **F.** She learned to take an engine apart and put it back together.

   ○ **G.** She avoided a sledding accident by being calm.

   ○ **H.** She learned how to fly at night.

   ● **J.** She set many flying records.

7. What information in the story helps you know that Amelia Earhart was fearless? *(making inferences)*

   ○ **A.** She got excited when she saw pilots doing tricks in the air.

   ● **B.** She flew across the Atlantic Ocean by herself.

   ○ **C.** She liked playing games.

   ○ **D.** She learned to fly.

**8.** Which of the following most likely helped Amelia Earhart to become a great pilot? *(cause and effect)*

- ● **F.** practicing flying
- ○ **G.** playing sports while growing up
- ○ **H.** watching airplanes do tricks
- ○ **J.** seeing her first plane at age 11

**9.** Why might someone consider Amelia Earhart a hero? *(comprehension/critical thinking)*

- ○ **A.** She could fix airplanes.
- ○ **B.** She learned how to fly at night.
- ● **C.** She was brave and did things no one had done before.
- ○ **D.** She was famous and traveled a lot.

Score for Items 5–9 (x 3) _____

15

You have just read about the adventures of Amelia Earhart. Now read a story about a boy who has had a different kind of adventure.

# Randy's Day to Remember

Randy and his father were soaking wet as they huddled close together under a tree. Thunder rumbled nearby. Streams of rain poured down the mountain trail.

The first two days of their camping trip had been perfect. But this morning the sky had turned dark and stormy. Randy's father had decided they should hike back down the mountain trail. They had not gone far when they were caught in a downpour. Now the trail was washed out. It was impossible to hike in the deep mud.

Suddenly, Randy heard an engine. "Do you hear that, Dad?"

Randy's father jumped to his feet. "That's a helicopter," he said. "They must be looking for hikers trapped by the storm. We've got to let them know where we are."

Randy and his father moved into an open area. They took off their bright orange raincoats and waved them in the air. Before long, the helicopter headed their way.

"They've spotted us!" said Randy's father. "They're going to pick us up."

Randy's heart beat faster as he watched the helicopter move into the clearing. The pilot waved down at them and dropped a rope ladder.

Tears ran down Randy's face as they approached safety. "What a wonderful job, being able to rescue people," he thought. "I want to learn how to fly a helicopter so I can help others too."

## Comparing Texts

**Write your answer to this question.**

10. In what **two** ways are Amelia Earhart and the helicopter pilot who rescued Randy and his father alike? *(comprehension/critical thinking)*

| Score | 0 | 2 | 4 |
|---|---|---|---|
| Criterion | Illegible, incorrect, or no answer | Answer provides only one accurate similarity. | Answer provides two accurate similarities. |
| Sample Answer | | *They were both pilots.* | *They were both pilots and they were both brave.* |

**Read each question and fill in the circle next to the best answer.**

11. Think about how Randy must have felt when the trail washed out. When might Amelia Earhart have felt the same way?
    *(making inferences)*

    ○ **F.** when she flew across the Atlantic Ocean

    ○ **G.** when she went to the Iowa State Fair

    ◉ **H.** when something went wrong on her last flight

    ○ **J.** when she set a new record

Rubric Score for Item 10 (x 1) _____
                                    4

*In considering a student's score, also feel free to give a score of 1 or 3, between those indicated above.*

**12** Integrated Theme Tests, Level 3 Theme 1: Off to Adventure!

**12.** Which event happens **after** the trail is washed out? *(sequence of events)*

&#9679; **A.** Randy hears a helicopter.

&#9675; **B.** Randy and his father begin to hike down the mountain.

&#9675; **C.** The morning sky turns dark.

&#9675; **D.** Randy and his father return to camp.

**13.** What helps the helicopter pilot find Randy and his father? *(cause and effect)*

&#9675; **F.** The rain stops.

&#9679; **G.** Randy and his father wave their orange raincoats.

&#9675; **H.** Randy and his father huddle under a tree.

&#9675; **J.** The pilot hears Randy and his father calling for help.

Score for Items 11–13 (x 3) _____
9

## ③ STRUCTURAL ANALYSIS AND VOCABULARY

**Read each question. Use what you know about figuring out words to help you select the correct answer.**

14. What is the meaning of the underlined word in the sentence below? *(base words, inflected endings)*

    Their parents <u>allowed</u> Amelia and Muriel to play baseball, football, and other sports.

    ○ **A.** told
    ○ **B.** paid
    ● **C.** let
    ○ **D.** helped

15. Which shows the correct way to divide the underlined word into syllables? *(syllabication)*

    And so Amelia began taking flying <u>lessons</u>.

    ○ **F.** less • ons
    ● **G.** les • sons
    ○ **H.** les • son • s
    ○ **J.** le • ssons

16. What does *trail* mean in the sentence below? *(multiple-meaning words)*

    Streams of rain poured down the mountain <u>trail</u>.

    ○ **A.** to fall behind
    ○ **B.** to follow the smell of something
    ○ **C.** a mark or path left by something that is moving
    ● **D.** a path through the woods

**17.** What does *record* mean in this sentence? *(multiple-meaning words)*

Amelia set more than one <u>record</u> in her little plane.

- ● **F.** the best official accomplishment in a category
- ○ **G.** to put away sound for future use
- ○ **H.** a person's history
- ○ **J.** to put in writing

**18.** What is the meaning of the underlined word in the sentence below? *(base words, inflected endings)*

"They've <u>spotted</u> us!" said Randy's father.

- ○ **A.** stained
- ○ **B.** having spots
- ○ **C.** surprised
- ● **D.** seen

Score for Items 14–18 (x 3) _____
                                 15

## [4] WRITING AND LANGUAGE

19. In Off to Adventure! you read about some exciting and unusual experiences. Think about something you did that you really enjoyed or that was exciting for you. Have you visited a new place or met someone exciting? Write a personal narrative about your experience.

Before you start writing, plan what you will say. You may want to use the organizer below or a separate sheet of paper.

| Who? Where? When? What? Chart | | | |
|---|---|---|---|
| Who? | Where? | When? | What? |
| | | | |

**When you write a personal narrative, remember to**
- write a beginning that grabs the reader's attention,
- include only the important events and tell them in order,
- include interesting details,
- write in your own voice, using *I*,
- keep to the topic,
- end in a way that finishes the story.

## Now write your personal narrative on the next page.

*Base each student's score only on the written personal narrative, not on the planning done, which is optional.*

## Scoring Rubric

| Score | 0 | 1 | 2 | 3 | 4 |
|-------|---|---|---|---|---|
| Criteria | Illegible or no answer | The narrative does not meet the criteria. The beginning and ending are difficult to decipher. Events are not important and are out of order. Only a few details are interesting. The author does not use his/her own voice. The author does not keep to the topic. There are multiple errors of all kinds. | The personal narrative minimally meets the criteria. Either the beginning or the ending does not do what it is supposed to. Many of the events are not important and are out of order. Most of the details are not interesting. The author struggles to keep to the topic. The author uses his/her own voice, but inconsistently. There are many errors, some simple ones. | The narrative generally meets the criteria. The beginning and ending are fine, but could be stronger. Events are important and told in order, but some details are not interesting. The author uses his/her own voice. The author may wander from the topic once or twice. There are a few grammar, spelling, and mechanics errors. | The personal narrative meets all the criteria. It has a strong beginning, and the ending completes the story. Only important events are included, and they are told in order. It is written in the author's own voice. The author keeps to the topic, making the narrative easy to follow. Any grammar, spelling, or mechanics errors are minor and infrequent. |

*On the following pages you will find sample student responses for Question 19.*

Rubric Score for Item 19 (x 6) $\dfrac{\phantom{XXXX}}{24}$

# Anchor Papers: *Sample Responses for Question 19*

**Score 4:** *This response has a strong beginning and ending and focuses on the prompt throughout. The writing is interesting and informative, and the narrative is easy to follow. There are almost no errors.*

The first time I rode a horse was the best day ever! I had never been on a horse before so my uncle said he would teach me. We went to a ranch. I got to ride on a gray horse named Dusty. It was so fun! I pulled on the reins to tell the horse which way to go or when to stop. I would also yell "Whoa!" when I wanted it to stop. I wish I could ride in a rodeo one day.

**Score 3:** *This narrative is interesting but lacks focus in places. Beginning and ending are in place, but neither is very strong. Some of the events are important. There are a few errors.*

My mom took me to see the ballet. I couldn't believe how high they jumped. The costumes were beautiful. My mom wanted me to take ballet lessons. The ballet told a story about a girl who got a nutcracker for a present. There were lots of different characters even mice. It was fun! I think it would be fun to be a dancer.

# Anchor Papers: *Sample Responses for Question 19*

**Score 2:** *This response has no beginning and a weak ending. Many of the events are not important, and there is minimal detail. The topic and use of personal voice wander. There are numerous errors.*

I could play football or basketball. My brothers team won the championship. He was the best and I went to every game. It is good to watch a lots of sports. I don't like baseball. I do exercise too. Then I will get picked for the NFL.

**Score 1:** *This response has no clear beginning and ending. Events are not important and there is very little detail. Author's own voice is not used, and topic is not in focus. Multiple errors make the narrative difficult to follow.*

It was at a birthday party when my brother was little and he could sing loud. There was a white dog that tried to sing and we laughed and we laughed really loud we had cake and chocolate and everyone said he sang loud.

**20.** Read the newspaper article below. Find and correct six errors. Use what you know about proofreading to make your corrections. The examples may help you. There are **three grammar errors** in sentences and subjects and predicates. There are also **three spelling errors.** *(short vowels a, e, i, o, u; vowel-consonant-e; what is a sentence?; kinds of sentences; subjects and predicates)*

## Finch Finishes Earhart's Flight

by Sylvia James — May 28, 1997

OAKLAND — Touching the plane down today in Oakland, California, Linda Finch ^made history. She left Oakland back in March with the hope of completing Amelia Earhart's flight around the world.

Sixty years ago, Ms. Earhart and her co-pilot, Mr. Noonan, disappeared over the Pacific Ocean. To this day, no one has been able to hunt down the plane's location. It was Ms. Finch's hope to ~~stike~~ ^stick to Ms. Earhart's original flight path. And ^she even used a plane just like Ms. Earhart's.

Upon landing today, Ms. Finch was greeted by a crowd that was as large and ~~wyde~~ ^wide as the field at the airport. She had wanted to show that Ms. Earhart's plan could work. She not only did that, but she also ^showed what it means not to give up on a dream.

*Base each student's score on the number of errors found and corrected, not on the student's use of proofreading marks. You may wish to refer students to the proofreading marks at the end of the* Practice Book *Student Handbook.*

Score for Item 20 (x 2) _____
                          12

**Read the following sentences.  Choose the sentence that shows the correct use of commas.**  *(using commas in dates and places)*

21.  ○ **A.** Amelia Earhart flew across the Atlantic on May, 20 1932.

 ○ **B.** Amelia Earhart flew across the Atlantic on May, 20, 1932.

 ○ **C.** Amelia Earhart flew across the Atlantic on, May 20, 1932.

 ◉ **D.** Amelia Earhart flew across the Atlantic on May 20, 1932.

**Read the following sentences.  Choose the sentence in which days of the week are shown correctly.**  *(capitalizing days and months)*

22.  ○ **F.** She went to flying lessons every tuesday and thursday.

 ○ **G.** She went to flying lessons every Tuesday and thursday.

 ◉ **H.** She went to flying lessons every Tuesday and Thursday.

 ○ **J.** She went to flying lessons every tuesday and Thursday.

Score for Items 21–22 (x 3) _____
6

## 5 LISTENING COMPREHENSION *(optional)*

**23.** *Ask students to listen carefully as you read aloud the following journal entry. Tell them that you will also read questions for them to answer. Then read aloud the journal entry and each question, allowing time for students to answer.*

> October 14, 1978
> Dear Diary,
>
> We have been climbing for ten days and are now near the top of the mountain. Tomorrow we will try to make the final climb to the top. No one thought that a group of women could climb this mountain, but now we are very close. I just hope there are no storms tomorrow.
>
> We packed our gear tonight and made sure we had everything we'd need. Tomorrow all we have to do is eat a good breakfast before we leave. Some of the group and our guides will stay behind to wait for our return to camp. It could take two more days to reach the top. There isn't much oxygen up here, so we have to move slowly. I've been preparing for tomorrow for a long time. I hope everything goes smoothly. I'll let you know when I get back.

*23. How would you feel if this were you on the mountain? Give two reasons why you would feel that way. (comprehension/critical thinking)*

| Score | 0 | 1 | 2 | 3 | 4 |
|---|---|---|---|---|---|
| Criterion | Illegible, unrelated, or no answer | Answers the question without supporting examples | Answers the question with unrelated examples | Answers the question with one related example | Answers the question with two related examples |
| Sample Answer | | *I would be excited.* | *I'd be excited because I like going for walks and I like writing in a journal.* | *I'd be scared because I don't like high places.* | *I'd be unhappy because I don't like heights and I don't like camping.* |

*24. What do climbers need to do when there is only a small amount of oxygen in the air?* *(cause and effect)*

**24.** ● **A.** move slowly

○ **B.** take deep breaths

○ **C.** leave their packs behind

○ **D.** eat a good breakfast

*25. Based on what you heard, how do you think the person who wrote this journal entry feels? (making inferences)*

**25.** ○ **F.** cold

● **G.** nervous

○ **H.** sick

○ **J.** confused

**6 POSTER** *Self-Assessment (optional)*

Think about what you have read and learned in *Off to Adventure!* Then fill in the poster.

**Theme Selections**
*Cliffhanger*
*The Ballad of Mulan*
*The Lost and Found*

I've been exploring adventure stories!

**My favorite story in this theme:**
_____
_____
_____

**Something new I found out:**
_____
_____
_____

**New words I can use:**
_____
_____
_____

**An adventure I would like to have:**
_____
_____
_____

# Celebrating Traditions

Level 3, Theme 2

## Integrated Theme Test Record

Student _____ Date _____

### Student Profile

| Part | Part Scores: | Excellent Progress | Good Progress | Some Progress | Needs Improvement |
|---|---|---|---|---|---|
| **1: Reading Strategy**<br>• evaluate | Items 1–2 | 7–8 | 5–6 | 3–4 | 0–2 |
| **2: Comprehension/Comparing Texts**<br>• author's viewpoint; categorize and classify; noting details; topic, main idea, and supporting details | Items 3–4, 10 (written) | 10–12 | 7–9 | 4–6 | 0–3 |
| | Items 5–9, 11–13 (multiple-choice) | 21–24 | 12–18 | 6–9 | 0–3 |
| **3: Structural Analysis and Vocabulary**<br>• compound words; plurals; contractions with 's, n't, 're, 'll; plurals with words ending in ch, sh, x, s<br>• word families, rhyming words | Items 14–19 | 15–18 | 9–12 | 6 | 0–3 |
| **4: Writing and Language**<br>Writing Fluency: Instructions | Item 20 Fluency | 24 | 18 | 12 | 0–6 |
| Proofreading<br>• more long vowel spellings, the long o sound, three-letter clusters and unexpected consonant patterns, the long i sound<br>• common nouns, proper nouns, singular and plural nouns, special plural nouns | Item 21 Language | 8 | 6 | 4 | 0–2 |
| Writing Skills<br>• correcting run-on sentences<br>• writing complete sentences | Items 22–23 | 6 | | 3 | 0 |
| **5: Listening Comprehension (optional)**<br>• author's viewpoint, categorize and classify, noting details | | Since the Listening Comprehension subtest is optional, it is not included in the total score. If you choose to give the subtest, evaluate answers for evidence of strengths and weaknesses. | | | |
| **6: Self-Assessment (optional)**<br>• self-assessment/reflection<br>• developing preferences | Poster | Scoring of Self-Assessment is not recommended. Evaluate answers for evidence of metacognitive growth. | | | |

**Total Score:** _____ /100

Test taken independently ☐
Test taken with partial support ☐
Test taken with full support ☐

Additional Comments _____

_____

_____

# PROVIDING SUPPORT

Most students should be able to take the test independently. For those needing more support, use the following suggestions.

## Partial Support

- Use one or both of these activities before students read:

---

**Prior Knowledge/Building Background**

Use the following ideas to spark discussion about the selection:
- Ask students if they have ever been to a fair. Have them describe what it was like.
- Ask students if they think an event like a fair would be fun.

---

**Purpose for Reading**

Have students read to find out what happens at a country fair.

---

- Allow students to read the selection cooperatively with a partner.
- Help students understand the questions and plan their answers.

## Full Support

- Use **Prior Knowledge/Building Background** and **Purpose for Reading** activities above.
- **Supported Reading** Have students read the selection in segments. After each segment, use the questions to support students' reading:

---

**Supported Reading**

Segment 1: From the beginning to the end of page 27
   Question: *What is happening at the fair?*
Segment 2: From the beginning of page 28 to the end of the selection
   Question: *Why does the author describe the day as perfect?*

---

- Encourage students to answer the test questions independently. If necessary, have them answer the questions orally in a group.
- For further support, have students work individually with you to answer the questions orally.

# Celebrating Traditions

In Celebrating Traditions you read about traditions that families share and enjoy year after year. Now you will read about a tradition shared by many families — a country fair. You will find out about the sights, sounds, games and contests, rides, and general fun that are part of the fair.

There are questions to answer during and after your reading. You may go back to the selection to help you answer the questions.

# COUNTRY FAIR

**by Gail Gibbons**

Hooray! It's opening day for the country fair! Cars and trucks begin to fill a farmer's field. People from all around head for the admission gate to buy their tickets. The high school marching band leads the way.

"Buy your cotton candy here!" a worker cries out as people enter the fairgrounds. *Oink . . . baa . . . moo . . .* Animal sounds fill the air.

Families and friends stroll down the midway looking at everything. Tents and stands fill both sides of this main route down the center of the fairground. There are games to play and much to see. "Test your skills!" a man yells from the ring-toss booth.

*Clang!* A very strong person just made the bell ring. Nearby, a bunch of kids throw balls at targets. Outside the bingo tent, a clown paints and decorates children's faces.

Refreshment stands full of popcorn, french fries, pizza, and fried dough are bustling with activity. Chicken sizzles on the grill, and there's a long line at the hamburger stand. "We make our own ice cream," a woman tells her customer proudly.

The Ferris wheel slowly turns, taking its passengers high up into the sky. A balloon floats by. What a view there is at the top! The merry-go-round plays a lively tune as the riders go up and down . . . up and down.

A line snakes in front of the Mad Mouse ride. Passengers on the ride shriek as they race around the track. Everyone loves the rides at the country fair!

 **Stop here and answer Question 1. Then continue reading.**

## **1** **READING STRATEGY**

1. **Evaluate** The author thinks that country fairs are fun. What are two ways that she helps you know that fairs are fun?

| Score | 0 | 1 | 2 | 3 | 4 |
|-------|---|---|---|---|---|
| Criterion | Illegible, unrelated, or no answer | Answer is loosely related to question. | Answer has one general example. | Answer has two general examples. | Answer has two specific examples. |
| Sample Answer | | *She describes animal noises.* | *She tells what rides there are.* | *She talks about rides and games.* | *She talks about kids playing games and people having fun on the rides.* |

Many country fairs celebrate the fall harvest. Inside the biggest exhibit hall, people display prized fruits and vegetables from their summer gardens. A row of pumpkins lines one wall, and tomatoes, squash, green beans, and other vegetables are on display as well. The best entry in each category is awarded a blue ribbon.

Home-canned vegetables and fruit line the shelves. There are jellies and jams, and maple syrup will be judged, too. People show off pies, cakes, muffins, and loaves of bread for prizes as well.

Flower arrangements look beautiful and smell like a real garden. A judge strolls by, deciding which rose display will win first prize. The tallest sunflower already has a blue ribbon attached to it.

Arts and crafts are on display in tents outside the exhibit halls. Paintings, sculptures, and photographs are being exhibited in one tent. And next door, one can see handmade crafts such as needlework, pillows, pottery, and quilts. "My quilt won a blue ribbon!" one girl says to her friend.

Outside, people look at the latest in farm equipment. "Have I got a deal for you!" one salesperson says to his customer.

Over at a fenced-in area, a calf judging is taking place. One by one, the calves parade through the center of the arena as the judges take notes. Some of these calves are owned by members of the Future Farmers of America or the 4-H club. They've brushed their calves' coats until they're bright and shiny. "The first-prize winner is . . ."

Other farm animals rest in their stalls, waiting their turn. The oxen are huge! One girl feeds her goats as sheep bleat, chickens cackle, and pigs squeal.

Not too far away, in another exhibit building, cows and calves moo, while outside, a pig-calling contest is going on. "Sooo-eee!" cries a little boy. Everyone cheers.

Next door is a model of a one-room schoolhouse. A little girl in overalls stands outside ringing the bell. Inside, a woman dressed up as an old-fashioned schoolteacher writes on a chalkboard and answers questions.

A fiddlers' contest is taking place outside the schoolhouse. Across the way, folks young and old demonstrate contra dancing. A man shouts out dance calls as the dancers swing around. The music plays, and everyone claps along to the beat.

As evening comes to the fair, the grandstand's lights flood the arena with brightness. A band plays country music. The seats fill up and everyone — young and old — sways to the music.

Now it is nighttime. The moon sits high in the sky. Fireworks light up the darkness, bursting into spectacular patterns. *Bang! Pop!* It's a perfect way to end a perfect day.

## Reading Strategy (continued)

2. **Evaluate** What words does the author use to make the evening and night seem like a good time? Give two examples.

| Score | 0 | 1 | 2 | 3 | 4 |
|---|---|---|---|---|---|
| Criterion | Illegible, unrelated, or no answer | Answer is loosely related to question. | Answer has one general example. | Answer has two general examples. | Answer has two specific examples. |
| Sample Answer | | *I like what happens at night.* | *She makes it seem like a good time because of the fireworks.* | *Music is playing, and there are fireworks.* | *She says everyone is dancing to the music and the fireworks are perfect.* |

## 2 COMPREHENSION

**Write your answers to these questions. Look back at the selection for help.**

3. Based on the first two paragraphs on page 25, how does the author feel about the fair? Give two examples that support your answer. *(author's viewpoint)*

| Score | 0 | 1 | 2 | 3 | 4 |
|---|---|---|---|---|---|
| Criterion | Illegible, unrelated, or no answer | Answer is vague and without supporting examples. | Answer is supported with only one general example. | Answer has two examples, but only one is specific. | Answer is supported with two specific examples. |
| Sample Answer | | *She likes fairs.* | *She feels the fair is fun. People show up from all over.* | *She feels it's fun. There is a band and someone is yelling.* | *She feels the fair is exciting because she says* Hooray! *and there is a band.* |

4. A main idea of *Country Fair* is that there are many things for children to do at a fair. Fill in the web below with two more details that support this idea. *(topic, main idea, and supporting details)*

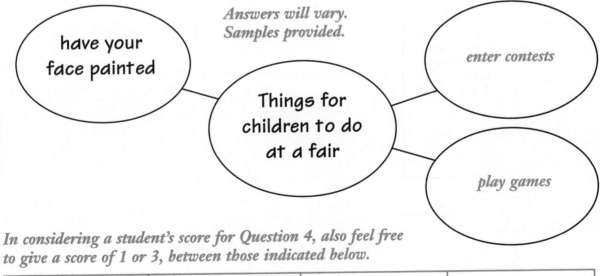

*Answers will vary. Samples provided.*

- have your face painted
- Things for children to do at a fair
- enter contests
- play games

*In considering a student's score for Question 4, also feel free to give a score of 1 or 3, between those indicated below.*

| Score | 0 | 2 | 4 |
|---|---|---|---|
| Criterion | Illegible, no answer, or entirely inaccurate | Provides one accurate supporting detail | Provides two accurate supporting details |

Rubric Score for Items 3–4 (x 1) ——— 8

**Read each question and fill in the circle next to the best answer. Look back at the selection for help.**

5. Which is a game that children play at the fair? *(categorize and classify)*

   ○ **A.** dancing
   ○ **B.** checkers
   ○ **C.** tag
   ● **D.** ringtoss

6. People enjoy many different kinds of food at the fair. Which one is **not** in the story? *(categorize and classify)*

   ● **F.** turkey
   ○ **G.** pizza
   ○ **H.** chicken
   ○ **J.** ice cream

7. What does the author think about riding the Ferris wheel?
   *(author's viewpoint)*

   ○ **A.** It's unsafe.
   ● **B.** It's exciting.
   ○ **C.** It's boring.
   ○ **D.** It moves too slowly.

8. For what things do people win blue ribbons at the fair?

*(noting details)*

- ○ **F.** the prettiest dress
- ◉ **G.** the smallest puppy
- ◉ **H.** the best flowers
- ○ **J.** the best hat

9. Why do you think people sell farm equipment at the country fair? *(noting details)*

- ◉ **A.** because farmers come to the fair
- ○ **B.** because the equipment is large
- ○ **C.** because children like to ride the equipment
- ○ **D.** because they want to enter the equipment in a contest

Score for Items 5–9 (x 3) ———
15

You just read about what it is like to go to a country fair. Now you will read about a family that carries on a special tradition at the country fair. There are questions to answer after you read.

# A Blue-Ribbon Secret

My name is Paula Simpson. Today is a big day for me. My family is hoping to win the barbecue contest at the fair. My great-grandfather created a special sauce more than one hundred years ago. He taught the recipe to his children, and my grandfather taught it to us. He didn't tell anyone except his family what was in it.

Every year at the fair, people line up at our table. They can't wait to taste our sauce. We won the barbecue contest two years ago. But last year, the Green family changed their recipe. Their new sauce was so good that it won the blue ribbon.

When that happened, my family spent months trying to improve our recipe. My great-grandfather's recipe calls for maple syrup, vinegar, tomato juice, and spices. We needed something else. I suggested that we add *peaches!* So we put two peaches in the blender, added the sauce, and mixed it until it was smooth. Our new sauce has a sweet and spicy flavor. It tastes better than ever!

Here come the judges now! The main judge is tasting our sauce. She's smiling! I'm hopeful that we have a blue-ribbon secret!

## Comparing Texts

**Write your answer to this question. Look back at *Country Fair* and "A Blue-Ribbon Secret" for help.** *(categorize and classify)*

10. What are two things that are the same about Paula's fair and the fair in the first story?

| Score | 0 | 2 | 4 |
|---|---|---|---|
| Criterion | Illegible, unrelated, or no answer | Correctly names one thing that is in both stories | Correctly names two things that are in both stories |
| Sample Answer | | *There are contests at both fairs.* | *People bring food they have made. Winners get blue ribbons.* |

**Read each question. Choose the best answer and fill in the circle.**

11. Which could be a main idea of **both** *Country Fair* and "A Blue-Ribbon Secret"? *(topic, main idea, and supporting details)*

    ○ **F.** Judging farm animals is an important part of a country fair.

    ○ **G.** Rides, contests, and music are all part of a country fair.

    ○ **H.** Families are proud of their secret barbecue recipes.

    ◉ **J.** Fairs are fun for families.

Rubric Score for Item 10 (x 1) _____
4

*In considering a student's score, also feel free to give a score of 1 or 3, between those indicated above.*

**12.** How does the author of the second story feel about her family's tradition? *(author's viewpoint)*

    ○ **A.** She is upset because they waste a lot of time working on the recipe.

    ○ **B.** She is embarrassed to do something so old-fashioned and boring.

    ◉ **C.** She is proud to have a secret family recipe that everyone likes.

    ○ **D.** She is angry because they lost the contest last year.

**13.** Why is Paula hopeful at the end of the story? *(noting details)*

    ○ **F.** She suggested they use peaches in the recipe.

    ◉ **G.** The judge looks happy.

    ○ **H.** Her great-grandfather created the recipe.

    ○ **J.** The sauce won a blue ribbon two years ago.

Score for Items 11–13 (x 3) _____
                              9

## ❸ STRUCTURAL ANALYSIS AND VOCABULARY

Read each question and the sentence after it. Use what you know about figuring out words to help you select the correct answers. Fill in the circle next to the best answer.

14. What is the base word for the underlined word in the sentence below? *(plurals with words ending in* ch, sh, x, s*)*

We put two <u>peaches</u> in the blender.

○ **A.** peache
⬤ **B.** peach
○ **C.** peachs
○ **D.** peachy

15. What does the underlined word in the sentence tell you about the crafts? *(compound words)*

<u>Handmade</u> crafts include pillows, pottery, and quilts.

⬤ **F.** They were made by hand.
○ **G.** They are in the shape of hands.
○ **H.** They have not been touched by hands.
○ **J.** They were made by machines.

16. What does the underlined word mean in the sentence below? *(contractions)*

He <u>didn't</u> tell anyone except his family what was in it.

○ **A.** does not
○ **B.** do not
⬤ **C.** did not
○ **D.** did

**17.** Which word is in the same word family as the two underlined words? *(word families)*

My family is <u>hoping</u> to win the barbecue contest.
I'm <u>hopeful</u> we have a blue-ribbon secret!

- ○ **F.** happiness
- ◉ **G.** hopeless
- ○ **H.** hopping
- ○ **J.** hopped

**18.** Which two words in this sentence rhyme? *(rhyming words)*

*The Ferris wheel slowly turns, taking its passengers high up into the sky.*

- ○ **A.** wheel, slowly
- ○ **B.** its, into
- ○ **C.** turns, passengers
- ◉ **D.** high, sky

**19.** What is the base word for the underlined word in the sentence below? *(plurals)*

*<u>Families</u> and friends stroll down the midway looking at everything.*

- ○ **F.** Familie
- ◉ **G.** Family
- ○ **H.** Famili
- ○ **J.** Familey

Score for Items 14–19 (x 3) _____
18

# 4 WRITING AND LANGUAGE *(instructions)*

**20.** In Celebrating Traditions you read about families sharing and passing down special ways of doing things. What has someone in your family or a friend taught you to do? Did you learn a new recipe or how to fix something? What steps were involved? How would you teach someone what you have learned? Write the instructions.

Before you start writing, plan what you will say. Use the chart below or a separate sheet of paper.

| Instructions for _____ | | |
|---|---|---|
| **First** | **Next** | **Finally** |
| _____ | _____ | _____ |
| _____ | _____ | _____ |
| _____ | _____ | _____ |
| _____ | _____ | _____ |
| _____ | _____ | _____ |

**When you write instructions, remember to**
- tell the purpose of the instructions and exactly what they are for,
- use a clear, step-by-step format,
- include time-order words and details in each step,
- end by saying again what your instructions are for.

## Now write your instructions on the next page.

*Base each student's score only on the written instructions, not on the planning done, which is optional.*

## Scoring Rubric

| Score | 0 | 1 | 2 | 3 | 4 |
|-------|---|---|---|---|---|
| Criterion | Illegible or no answer | The response does not meet the minimal criteria. There is no stated purpose. Steps are given out of order and not explained in detail. Major errors make the piece difficult to understand. | The response meets the criteria only minimally. The purpose is not clearly stated. Major errors in sequence make the steps difficult to follow. The steps lack detail and are vague. The purpose is not restated. | The response generally meets the criteria. The purpose is stated but needs to be more explicit. The basic steps are included with some time-order words, but may still be a bit unclear or out of order. The goal is restated but is vague. | The response meets all the criteria. The purpose is clear and well stated. The steps are organized in an easy-to-follow sequence and time-order words are used effectively. The goal is restated clearly at the end. |

*On the following pages you will find sample student responses for Question 20.*

Rubric Score for Item 20 (x 6) _____
$$\frac{}{24}$$

# Anchor Papers: *Sample Responses for Question 20*

**Score 4:** *This response has a clearly stated purpose. The steps are well organized and explained in detail. There are almost no errors in grammar and mechanics.*

> Here's how to grow your own tomatoes. First, tomatoes grow in the summer, so you'll want to plant them in the spring. When it's time, dig a small hole in the ground, about a quarter of an inch deep. Next, drop the seed in the hole and cover it with dirt. Then, water it and sit back and watch it grow. Every few days water it so the ground is damp. Finally, after about two months see if they are ready to be picked. First, check to see if they are red all the way around. Then check to see if they feel firm. If they are, then pick them, wash them, and eat your own tomatoes!

**Score 3:** *While its purpose could be stated more clearly, this response succeeds in explaining the steps in the process. Some steps are out of order and others could be more clearly explained. There are few errors in grammar and mechanics.*

> Don't worry, cooking eggs is pretty easy. First, get all the ingredients. Next, crack two eggs and a bowl and stir them up with a fork. You can put milk in too. Then you are ready to pour them in the pan to cook. Put butter in the pan and melt it. Let the eggs start to get a little bit cooked. Then you can stir them and turn them over to cook the other side. It's time to put them on a plate and have a delicious breakfast.

# Anchor Papers: *Sample Responses for Question 20*

**Score 2:** *This response has an unclear purpose. Some steps are left out and others are vague. The steps are difficult to follow, and there are numerous grammar and mechanics errors.*

My grandpa said come over and I came over and we were going to build with wood. He cut the boards and you could see the little knotholes and that's not where you should put a nail. It looked like a little house and it was a house for a bird. I held the boards and he put in the nail. I put on glue and I put some nails too. We're going to get some birdseed too.

**Score 1:** *This response has no purpose and is disorganized. Too few steps are given, and those that are have no explanation. The grammar and mechanics errors make the writing difficult to comprehend.*

I wanted another one because it was fun to put icing and sprinkles. I did every color and I ate it. It was a cupcake.

**21.** Read the announcement below. Find and correct four errors. Use what you know about proofreading to make your corrections. The examples may help you. There are a total of **two grammar errors** in proper nouns and special plural nouns. There are also **two spelling errors.**

*(more long vowel spellings, the long o sound, three-letter clusters and unexpected consonant patterns, the long i sound, common nouns, proper nouns, singular and plural nouns, special plural nouns)*

---

## Attention, Please!

Before you all leave, the Judges would like to announce the winner of our final contest.

May I have the envelope please? And it's a tie. Peter, with his horse, wesley, and Kit, with her horse, Alta, both win a blue ribbon!

Well, that does it. Please be careful driving home. Main Street will be crowded with folks just like you. And ladies and gentleman, please take all your boxes with you. Thank you, and see you all next year!

---

*Base each student's score on the number of errors found and corrected, not on the student's use of proofreading marks. You may wish to refer students to the proofreading marks at the end of the* Practice Book *Student Handbook.*

Score for Item 21 (x 2) _____
                          8

**22.** What is the best way to correct the run-on sentence below?

*(correcting run-on sentences)*

The games are my favorite part of the fair ball throwing is the best.

- ○ **A.** The games are my favorite part of the fair. ball throwing is the best.
- ○ **B.** The games are my favorite part of the fair, ball throwing is the best.
- ○ **C.** The games are my favorite part of the fair Ball throwing is the best.
- ● **D.** The games are my favorite part of the fair. Ball throwing is the best.

**23.** Which of the following is a complete sentence?

*(writing complete sentences)*

- ○ **F.** The judge on the best quilt a blue ribbon.
- ● **G.** The judge put a blue ribbon on the best quilt.
- ○ **H.** A blue ribbon on the best quilt.
- ○ **J.** A blue ribbon on the best quilt by the judge.

Score for Items 22–23 (x 3) _____
6

## ⑤ LISTENING COMPREHENSION *(optional)*

**24.** *Ask students to listen carefully as you read aloud the following announcement and each question. Allow time for students to answer each one.*

> "Now, boys and girls, listen up please!" said Mr. Nash. "Though we go to the zoo every year when we study animals, there are still some things I need to say. Listen carefully."
>
> "First, stay with your buddy at all times so you will have someone to look out for you. Second, don't feed the animals. Your food is not good for them. Third, keep your fingers out of the cages. And finally, if you get lost, look for a zookeeper to help you. Don't talk to strangers."
>
> "Are we ready? Good. Let's go!"

*24. Why does Mr. Nash tell the children all these things? Explain your answer. (author's viewpoint)*

| Score | 0 | 1 | 2 | 3 | 4 |
|---|---|---|---|---|---|
| Criterion | Illegible, unrelated, or no answer | Response recalls a general fact. | Response recalls a specific fact. | Response expresses a viewpoint that is somewhat accurate. | Response expresses a general, accurate viewpoint. |
| Sample Answer | | He wants to tell everyone that they are going to the zoo. | He wants to tell people not to put their fingers in cages. | He wants them to know how to behave. | He wants the children to be safe at the zoo. |

*25. Who most likely is Mr. Nash, the person talking? (noting details)*

**25.** ○ **A.** a parent

◉ **B.** a teacher

○ **C.** a student

○ **D.** a zookeeper

*26. What is the best way to describe the information in the announcement?*
*(categorize and classify)*

**26.** ○ **F.** trips to zoos

○ **G.** problems with animals

◉ **H.** rules to follow

○ **J.** ways to have fun

**6 POSTER** *Self-Assessment (optional)*

Complete the sentences about the theme Celebrating Traditions. Your responses should show that you have thought about what you have read.

**Theme Selections**

*The Keeping Quilt*
*Grandma's Records*
*The Talking Cloth*
*Dancing Rainbows*

**My favorite story in this theme is**

_____
_____
_____
_____
_____

**A new tradition I learned about is**

_____
_____
_____
_____

**Traditions**

**Some new words I learned are**

_____
_____
_____
_____
_____

**A tradition I like is**

_____
_____
_____
_____

# Incredible Stories

Level 3, Theme 3

## Integrated Theme Test Record

Student _____     Date _____

## Student Profile

| Part | Part Scores: | Excellent Progress | Good Progress | Some Progress | Needs Improve-ment |
|---|---|---|---|---|---|
| **1: Reading Strategy**<br>• question | Items 1–2 | 7–8 | 5–6 | 3–4 | 0–2 |
| **2: Comprehension/Comparing Texts**<br>• fantasy and realism, following directions, drawing conclusions, story structure | Items 3–4, 10 (written) | 10–12 | 7–9 | 4–6 | 0–3 |
| | Items 5–9, 11–13 (multiple-choice) | 21–24 | 12–18 | 6–9 | 0–3 |
| **3: Structural Analysis and Vocabulary**<br>• plurals of nouns ending in *f* or *fe*, word endings -*er* and -*est*, suffixes -*y* and -*ly*, prefixes *un*-, *dis*-, and *non*-<br>• using context | Items 14–19 | 15–18 | 9–12 | 6 | 0–3 |
| **4: Writing and Language**<br>Writing Fluency: Story<br>Proofreading<br>• vowel sounds in *clown* and *lawn*; vowel +/r/ sounds; /j/, /k/, and /kw/ sounds; homophones<br>• possessive nouns; what is a verb?; present time; past time and future time<br>Writing Skills<br>• using commas for direct address<br>• capitalization and punctuation with quotations | Item 20 Fluency | 24 | 18 | 12 | 0–6 |
| | Item 21 Language | 8 | 6 | 4 | 0–2 |
| | Items 22–23 Writing Skills | 6 | | 3 | 0 |
| **5: Listening Comprehension (optional)**<br>• fantasy and realism, following directions, drawing conclusions | | Since the Listening Comprehension subtest is optional, it is not included in the total score. If you choose to give the subtest, evaluate answers for evidence of strengths and weaknesses. | | | |
| **6: Self-Assessment (optional)**<br>• self-assessment/reflection<br>• developing preferences | Home Letter | Scoring of Self-Assessment is not recommended. Evaluate answers for evidence of metacognitive growth. | | | |

**Total Score:** _____ /100

Test taken independently ☐
Test taken with partial support ☐
Test taken with full support ☐

Additional Comments _____

_____

# PROVIDING SUPPORT

Most students should be able to take the test independently. For those needing more support, use the following suggestions.

## Partial Support

- Use one or both of these activities before students read:

---

**Prior Knowledge/Building Background**

Use the following ideas to spark discussion about the selection:
- Ask students what they would do with a noodle that lasts forever.
- Ask students to describe fantasy elements they have read in stories.

---

**Purpose for Reading**

Have students read to find out how a woman named Mama Lioni uses a noodle that lasts forever.

---

- Allow students to read the selection cooperatively with a partner.
- Help students understand the questions and plan their answers.

## Full Support

- Use **Prior Knowledge/Building Background** and **Purpose for Reading** activities above.
- **Supported Reading** Have students read the selection in segments. After each segment, use the questions to support students' reading:

---

**Supported Reading**

Segment 1: From the beginning to the end of page 50
   Questions: *Why is Mama Lioni's noodle so special? What are some things she does with it?*
Segment 2: From the beginning of page 51 to the end of the selection
   Questions: *How do the thieves get caught? What does Mama Lioni do with the reward?*

---

- Encourage students to answer the test questions independently. If necessary, have them answer the questions orally in a group.
- For further support, have students work individually with you to answer the questions orally.

# Incredible STORIES

In Incredible Stories you read stories that could not really happen, but which also had some real-life details in them. Now you will read about an old widow (a woman whose husband has died) who saves her town with the help of an amazing, everlasting noodle.

There are questions to answer before and during your reading. You may go back to the selection to help you answer the questions.

# Mama Lioni's Everlasting Noodle

**from *Spider* magazine
by Marcia Vaughan**

High in the hills of Tortona, a town in northern Italy, lived a widow called Mama Lioni. She was as old as the trees, as wise as an owl, and as poor as an empty pocket. But Mama Lioni was happy. She loved to eat noodle soup, and she had a big basket of noodles by the fireplace in her kitchen.

Each morning Mama Lioni reached into the basket and pulled out one long, straight noodle. She dropped the noodle into a pot of water and boiled up enough noodle soup to last all day.

One morning Mama Lioni reached into the basket and pulled out the very last noodle. This one wasn't long and straight; it was short and twisted.

"What will I eat when this noodle is gone?" wondered Mama Lioni, holding the strange little noodle in her hand. With a sigh, she dropped it into the pot.

But Mama Lioni had no need to worry, for that noodle was an *everlasting* noodle!

At once the noodle began to sputter and stretch and swell and swirl. It grew longer and longer and longer. Mama Lioni watched in awe as the noodle filled the pot, slithered over the side, and charged from the fireplace like a streak of lightning.

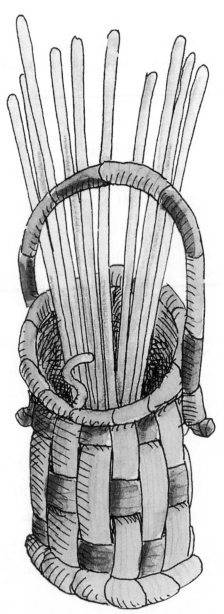

That noodle flipped and flopped and slipped and slopped around the room. It twisted up the table, wound around the windows, curled up in the corners, and wrapped itself around the rafters.

The noodle was about to climb up the chimney when Mama Lioni put out the fire. The noodle stopped growing.

Mama Lioni, licking her lips, cried, "This is the longest noodle I've ever cooked."

Mama Lioni sat down and began to eat the everlasting noodle. She gobbled and slurped and gulped and burped until she was as plump as a pumpkin. But there was still more noodle left than she could ever eat.

She sighed, "I must do something else with this noodle, or I shall pop!"

So Mama Lioni hung her washing from a length of noodle. She flew a kite from the hilltop. She skipped rope. She fenced her garden.

Exhausted, she sat down and began knitting the noodle into caps. She stitched it into trousers, spun it into scarves, crocheted it into vests, and wove it into jackets.

By evening Mama Lioni had made three complete noodle suits. One was long. One was short. And one was as round as an onion. She dyed the suits in beet, blueberry, and dandelion juice and hung them up to dry.

Mama Lioni danced with joy. "Tomorrow I will take these suits to market in Tortona and sell them for hundreds of lire!"

**STOP** Stop here and answer Question 1. Then continue reading.

---

## 1 READING STRATEGY

1. **Question** What is an important question about the story up to this point?

| Score | 0 | 2 | 4 |
|---|---|---|---|
| Criterion | Illegible, unrelated, or no answer | Asks about an unimportant detail | Asks about information that is central to the story |
| Sample Answer | | *Where does Mama Lioni keep the noodles?* | *What is special about that last noodle?* |

*In considering a student's score, also feel free to give a score of 1 or 3, between those indicated above.*

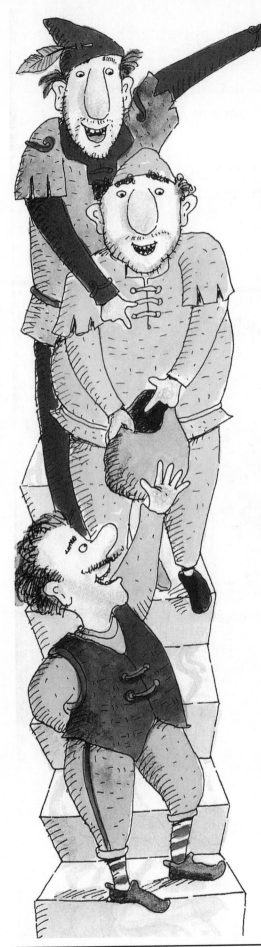

But early the next morning, three scheming thieves came sneaking up the hill and into Mama Lioni's house.

"Wake up, old mother, and give us your gold," said the tall thief, whose name was Caruso.

"I do not have any gold," said Mama Lioni, clutching her blankets.

"Then give us your jewels," snorted the short thief, whose name was Gubbio.

"I do not have any jewels, either," she answered.

"Then what do you have?" scowled Luigi, who was as round and smelly as an onion. "We are thieves, after all, and must steal *something!*"

Mama Lioni thought. "All I have," she said, pointing out the window, "are those."

"What remarkable clothes!" cried Caruso when he saw the noodle suits blowing in the breeze.

"Dressed in those, we would look like noblemen," Gubbio agreed.

"Noblemen sent to collect taxes from the villagers of Tortona," Luigi cried, rubbing his dirty hands together with glee.

So the three thieves dressed in the noodle suits, marched into Tortona, and climbed the steps of the town hall.

"We are Lord Mayor Marzollo's tax collectors," Caruso announced to the villagers. "Give us all your gold."

"Give us all your jewels!" shouted Gubbio.

"Give us all you've got!" Luigi added, passing a bag around. Trusting such well-dressed noblemen, the good people of Tortona dropped all their valuables into the bag.

But the thieves wanted more.

"Give us your food!" cried Caruso.

"Give us your animals!" roared Gubbio.

"Give us all your — " No one heard what Luigi said, for at that moment a bolt of lightning split the sky, and rain tumbled down like a waterfall.

The thieves took no notice of the downpour. But noodle suits are not meant to be worn in the rain. When noodles get wet, they get soggy.

Those noodles began to sag and bag and stretch. And as the rain kept falling, so did the noodle suits.

"Those are not tax collectors," roared the crowd, "they are thieves! Catch them!"

Caruso, Gubbio, and Luigi tried to run away. But the tangle of noodles around their feet tripped them up, and they fell in a sloppy heap.

The villagers' gold and jewels were returned. The three thieves were sentenced to slice onions in the jail kitchen. And with her reward, Mama Lioni built a handsome home for all the poor orphans of Tortona.

After all, she had an everlasting noodle. What more could she want?

## READING STRATEGY (continued)

2. **Question** What is an important question about the story you can ask?

| Score | 0 | 2 | 4 |
|---|---|---|---|
| Criterion | Illegible, unrelated, or no answer | Asks about an unimportant detail | Asks about information that is central to the story |
| Sample Answer | | *What does Luigi look like?* | *How are the thieves caught?* |

*In considering a student's score, also feel free to give a score of 1 or 3, between those indicated above.*

Rubric Score for Items 1–2 (x 1) ——— 8

## 2 COMPREHENSION

**Write your answers to these questions. Look back at the selection for help.**

3. Think about the many ways Mama Lioni uses the noodle. What does this tell you about the kind of person she is? Explain your answer. *(drawing conclusions)*

| Score | 0 | 1 | 2 | 3 | 4 |
|---|---|---|---|---|---|
| Criterion | Illegible, unrelated, or no answer | Makes a vague conclusion that essentially restates a fact from the story | Draws a conclusion, but it doesn't describe character | Draws an accurate conclusion, but the explanation is lacking | Draws an accurate conclusion and explains it clearly |
| Sample Answer | | *Mama Lioni is a person who likes noodle soup.* | *She lives by herself so she has to do everything herself.* | *The many ways Mama Lioni uses the noodle show that she can take care of herself.* | *Mama Lioni can take care of herself. She cooks, makes clothes, flies kites, and builds a fence with the noodle.* |

4. Fill in the chart to tell how the problem in "Mama Lioni's Everlasting Noodle" is solved at the end. *(story structure)*

| Score | 0 | 2 | 4 |
|---|---|---|---|
| Criterion | Illegible or no answer | Explanation is unclear or only partially correct | Thoroughly explains how problem is solved |
| Sample Answer | | *The thieves ask for money. It rains and their suits fall off. Everyone is happy.* | *The thieves go into town and ask for everyone's valuables. Then it rains and their noodle suits get soggy and fall off. The people in the town catch the thieves and get their gold and jewels back. Mama Lioni gets a reward.* |

*In considering a student's score, also feel free to give a score of 1 or 3, between those indicated above.*

Rubric Score for Items 3–4 (x 1) _____
8

**Read each question. Choose the best answer and fill in the circle.**

5. According to the story, which is something you need to make noodle soup? *(following directions)*

   ○ **A.** a basket
   ○ **B.** lots of time
   ● **C.** boiling water
   ○ **D.** lots of noodles

6. Why does Mama Lioni give the thieves the clothes she had made? *(drawing conclusions)*

   ● **F.** There is nothing else for the thieves to steal.
   ○ **G.** She feels sorry for the thieves.
   ○ **H.** They need clothes.
   ○ **J.** She does not like the thieves.

7. Why are the people of the town happy at the end of the story? *(story structure)*

   ○ **A.** Mama Lioni's suits are returned to her.
   ○ **B.** It begins to rain.
   ○ **C.** The thieves are nice people.
   ● **D.** Their gold and jewels are returned to them.

8. Which of these events happen in the story but **could not** happen in real life? *(fantasy and realism)*

- ○ **F.** Mama Lioni makes soup with noodles.
- ● **G.** The noodle keeps growing.
- ○ **H.** Mama Lioni flies up in the sky.
- ○ **J.** The thieves rob Mama Lioni.

9. Which of these events happen in the story and **could** happen in real life? *(fantasy and realism)*

- ○ **A.** Clothes hang from a noodle.
- ○ **B.** Someone pops from eating too much.
- ● **C.** Someone makes noodle soup.
- ○ **D.** A noodle is used to skip rope.

Score for Items 5–9 (x 3) _____

15

You just read about a woman who makes soup and suits from noodles. The story below includes a recipe for noodle soup. Read the story and then answer the questions that follow it.

# Nifty Noodle Soup

Samantha walked into her father's office. "Hey, Dad, are you working late again?"

"Yup. It's a busy time of year, Sam."

"Can I make you dinner?"

"That's very nice of you to offer. I don't have time to cook these days," he replied. "How about some of that nifty noodle soup? I think the recipe is in the box on the counter. Thanks, Sam."

"You're welcome."

Samantha walked into the kitchen, found the recipe, and began reading the directions to herself. "It says I need two tablespoons of butter, one cup of chopped vegetables, and a quart of boiling water. I also need a tablespoon of parsley, one bay leaf, salt and pepper, and one cup of uncooked noodles.

"First, I heat the butter in a pot until it is melted. Second, I add the vegetables and cook these for five minutes. Next, the recipe says to add the water and boil the vegetables gently for thirty minutes. Once this is done, the spices are added and then the noodles. Everything is cooked for ten more minutes. It is supposed to make enough for two people. This doesn't look too difficult."

"Dinner will be ready in forty-five minutes, Dad," Samantha called out.

# Comparing Texts

**Write your answers to these questions. Look back at "Mama Lioni's Everlasting Noodle" and "Nifty Noodle Soup" for help.**

**10.** What do you think would happen to Samantha's soup if she used Mama Lioni's noodle? Explain your answer.

*(comprehension/critical thinking)*

| Score | 0 | 1 | 2 | 3 | 4 |
|---|---|---|---|---|---|
| Criterion | Illegible, unrelated, incorrect, or no answer | Answer includes element of fantasy not in the first story. | Answer is accurate but vague and needs explanation. | Answer is accurate, but explanation is vague. | Answer is accurate and thoroughly explained. |
| Sample Answer | | *The noodles in the second story would talk.* | *There would be a strange noodle in her soup.* | *The noodles in the girl's soup would last forever. She and her father would be happy.* | *The girl's noodles would be everlasting like Mama Lioni's. Then she wouldn't have to make dinner again.* |

**Read each question. Choose the best answer and fill in the circle.**

**11.** How are Mama Lioni's and Samantha's noodle soups the same?

*(following directions)*

&#9675; **A.** Only one noodle is needed.

&#9679; **B.** The noodles are placed in a pot of water.

&#9675; **C.** Vegetables are used.

&#9675; **D.** The recipe makes enough to last the whole day.

Rubric Score for Item 10 (x 1) _____
4

**12.** Where does Samantha's father have his office? *(drawing conclusions)*

○ **F.** in Tortona, Italy
○ **G.** outside
● **H.** in their home
○ **J.** in a big building

**13.** What is the problem in "Nifty Noodle Soup"? *(story structure)*

● **A.** Samantha's father is too busy to cook.
○ **B.** Samantha doesn't understand the directions.
○ **C.** Samantha tells her father that dinner will be ready in forty-five minutes.
○ **D.** Samantha cannot find the ingredients.

Score for Items 11–13 (x 3) _____
9

# 3 STRUCTURAL ANALYSIS AND VOCABULARY

**Read the sentences. Use what you know about figuring out words to help you select the correct answers.**

14. I also need one cup of <u>uncooked</u> noodles.

    What kind of noodles are needed?  *(prefixes un-, dis-, non-)*

    ○ **F.** noodles that are already cooked
    ◉ **G.** noodles that are not yet cooked
    ○ **H.** noodles that are soft
    ○ **J.** noodles that do not need to be cooked

15. *"We are <u>thieves</u> after all."*

    What are thieves?  *(plurals of nouns ending in f or fe)*

    ○ **A.** people who cook
    ○ **B.** people who knit
    ◉ **C.** people who steal
    ○ **D.** people who are honest

16. *"This is the <u>longest</u> noodle I've ever cooked," said Mama Lioni.*

    What surprised Mama Lioni about the noodle?  *(word endings er and est)*

    ○ **F.** It was tasty.
    ◉ **G.** It was long.
    ○ **H.** It was soft.
    ○ **J.** It was short.

**17.** Mama Lioni <u>skips</u> rope with the noodle.

What does Mama Lioni do with the noodle? *(using context)*

- ● **A.** She jumps over the noodle.
- ○ **B.** She watches the noodle hop and jump.
- ○ **C.** She throws the noodle into the air.
- ○ **D.** She doesn't do anything with the noodle.

**18.** What is the meaning of the underlined word in the sentence below? *(suffixes -y and -ly)*

Luigi was as round and <u>smelly</u> as an onion.

- ○ **F.** smells the most
- ● **G.** full of smell
- ○ **H.** in a way that smells
- ○ **J.** the opposite of smell

**19.** The thieves could have used <u>nonskid</u> soles on their shoes.

What kind of soles could the thieves have used? *(prefixes un-, dis-, non-)*

- ○ **A.** soles that slip more than most
- ○ **B.** soles that slip the most of all
- ○ **C.** soles that slip only a little
- ● **D.** soles that do not slip at all

Score for Items 14–19 (x 3) _____
18

## 4 WRITING AND LANGUAGE

*(story)*

**20.** In Incredible Stories you read stories with both realistic and make-believe details. Now you will write a real or make-believe story of your own. Are the main characters people or talking animals? Does the story take place in your home or on another planet? Could the events in your story really happen?

Before you start writing, you may use the chart below to help you plan your story. Use a separate sheet of paper if you need more room.

| Main Characters | Setting |
|---|---|
|  |  |

| Plot | |
|---|---|
| **Beginning** | **Ending** |
|  |  |

**When you write a story, remember to**
- introduce the characters, setting, and problem at the beginning,
- tell the story events in order,
- use interesting details to describe the characters and setting,
- write an ending that wraps up the story.

## Now write your story on the next page.

*Base each student's score only on the written story, not on the planning done, which is optional.*

## Scoring Rubric

| Score | 0 | 1 | 2 | 3 | 4 |
|---|---|---|---|---|---|
| **Criterion** | Illegible or no answer | Story does not meet the minimal criteria. Characters and setting are not introduced or described. The story events are confusing, with no sense of plot. Few details are given. The ending is missing. Major errors exist. | Story meets the criteria only minimally. Characters and setting are only vaguely introduced or described. The story events are unclear and out of order. Some plot details are irrelevant. The ending is there, but it is weak. There are many errors. | Story generally meets the criteria. Characters and setting are introduced but need more elaboration. The story events are presented in order, but plot needs more development. Details provide some sense of character. The ending basically wraps up the story. There are some errors. | Story meets all the criteria. The characters and setting are well developed in the beginning with strong details. The story events are clear and detailed. Details enhance the characters. The ending nicely wraps up the story. There are few, if any, errors. |

*On the following pages you will find sample student responses for Question 20.*

Rubric Score for Item 20 (x 6) _____
24

# Anchor Papers: *Sample Responses for Question 20*

**Score 4:** *This story has a strong beginning, middle, and end. The characters and setting are described in detail, and dialogue is used effectively. There are almost no errors in grammar, spelling, and mechanics.*

Once there was a sad little unicorn. He lived in the Candy Kingdom where everything was made of candy. He was sad because he was the only unicorn in the kingdom and there was no one to play with. One day, he was standing by a lollipop tree crying. "If only I had a friend," he cried. "We could go to the candy beach and make sugar sand castles because the sand is sugar." Suddenly he heard a nice, soft voice. "I'm a unicorn, too," it said. "I can be your friend." The little unicorn was so happy that he ran around and around in a circle. The two friends built an enormous sugar sand castle where they could live. The two little unicorns were never lonely again.

**Score 3:** *This story has a beginning, middle, and end, though the end is weak. Characters and setting are introduced but need to be more fully described. There are some errors in grammar, spelling, and mechanics.*

One morning I woke up and my bed looked different. It had wings!!! I said "Go to the north pole" and it did. I was at the north pole! I met a baby polar bear and we made friends. He said "Do you know how to ride a sled?" I said no and he said "We can make your bed be a sled." My bed turned into a sled and we had lots of fun riding down the hills. I said "I have to go home. Do you want to come?" The polar bear said he wanted to stay in the snow at the north pole. So my bed went home and didn't have wings anymore.

# Anchor Papers: *Sample Responses for Question 20*

**Score 2:** *This story has an abrupt beginning and ending. Characters are randomly introduced, and there are few details to clarify who they are. The plot is repetitious and disconnected. There are a number of errors in grammar, spelling, and mechanics.*

A giraffe came in my room and was talking. Then a baboon came in too. Then he wanted to play checkers. My brother and all my friends came over and couldn't believe it. Then an elephant came and we all rode on it. My mom told us to clean up because there was a mess from all those talking animals. Then a parrot came and said it could talk before the other animals did. It could always talk. Then they all went back to the jungle.

**Score 1:** *This response does not have a beginning or end. The characters are not identified, and the plot is undeveloped. The grammar, spelling, and mechanics errors make the writing difficult to comprehend.*

It was a scary thing. It was snoring but it wasn't sleeping. They ran and saw it and screamed. It was scared too and screamed. One said to come to dinner. Then everyone was friends. The end.

**21.** Read the letter below. Find and correct four errors. Use what you know about proofreading to make your corrections. The examples may help you. There are a total of **two grammar errors** in possessive nouns and verb tense. There are also **two spelling errors.**

*(vowel sounds in* clown *and* lawn; *vowel + /r/ sounds; /j/, /k/, and /kw/ sounds; homophones; possessive nouns; what is a verb?; present time; past time and future time)*

---

Dear Ms. Fletcher,

      will be
I ~~was~~ absent from school for the next four days. I

returned from your trip up north last night. When I wake
                                              o
                   k
up this morning, my scin was covered with noodles! I looked

in the mirror and saw that my hair had ahlso turned to

noodles!

    So you see, I must stay home so I won't get anyone

else sick. Please check the other students hair and arms.

I hope no one else has this noodle sickness.

                        Sincerely,

                        Tony

---

*Base each student's score on the number of errors found and corrected, not on the student's use of proofreading marks. You may wish to refer students to the proofreading marks at the end of the* Practice Book *Student Handbook.*

Score for Item 21 (x 2) _____
                      8

**22.** Choose the sentence that shows the correct use of commas. *(using commas for direct address)*

⬤ **A.** Wake up, Hector, or you'll miss the bus!

◯ **B.** Wake up Hector, or you'll miss the bus!

◯ **C.** Wake up, Hector or you'll miss the bus!

◯ **D.** Wake up Hector or you'll miss the bus!

**23.** Choose the sentence with correct capitalization and punctuation. *(capitalization and punctuation with quotations)*

◯ **F.** "You cannot have dessert," said the mother. "Until you finish eating your vegetables."

◯ **G.** "You cannot have dessert." said the mother, "until you finish eating your vegetables."

⬤ **H.** "You cannot have dessert," said the mother, "until you finish eating your vegetables."

◯ **J.** "You cannot have dessert," said the mother, "Until you finish eating your vegetables."

Score for Items 22–23 (x 3) _____
6

## 5 LISTENING COMPREHENSION *(optional)*

**24.** *Ask students to listen carefully as you read aloud the following story. Tell them that you will also read questions for them to answer. Then read aloud the story and each question, allowing time for students to answer.*

Mother poured some of her chicken noodle soup into a Thermos bottle and capped it tightly. She handed the Thermos bottle to her teenage son, Jesse.

"Please take this to Aunt Anne," said Mother. "Put it in your backpack along with the cookies you baked her. Be sure to pick up her medicine along the way. And please remind Aunt Anne that her doctor's appointment is tomorrow morning at nine o'clock."

Jesse packed up the food and stepped out the back door. He hopped on his bike and began the ride into town.

*24. What problem would you add to make the story plot more interesting? Explain how this changes the story. (story structure)*

| Score | 0 | 1 | 2 | 3 | 4 |
|---|---|---|---|---|---|
| Criterion | Illegible or no answer | Unrelated, or mistakes characters or setting for plot problem | Adds a problem to the plot, but gives no explanation | Adds an interesting problem to the plot, but explanation is not thorough | Adds a logical problem to the plot and accurately explains how it will change the story |
| Sample Answer | | *Jesse rides a dirt bike.* | *Jesse forgets to pick up the medicine.* | *Jesse gets lost and doesn't make it to his aunt's house.* | *Jesse eats the cookies on the way. Aunt Anne doesn't have enough to eat so Jesse cooks her lunch.* |

*25. What can you conclude about Aunt Anne? (drawing conclusions)*

**25.** ○ **A.** Her stove is broken.

⬤ **B.** She is sick.

○ **C.** She is a nurse.

○ **D.** She doesn't have time to cook.

*26. Which will happen if Jesse follows his mother's directions? (following directions)*

**26.** ○ **F.** Aunt Anne will miss her doctor's appointment.

○ **G.** Jesse will forget the cookies.

⬤ **H.** Aunt Anne will get her medicine.

○ **J.** Jesse will get lost.

## 6 HOME LETTER
*Self-Assessment (optional)*

**Write a letter to a friend or relative. Your letter should show that you have thought about what you have read.**

**Theme Selections**

*Dogzilla*
*The Mysterious Giant of Barletta*
*Raising Dragons*
*The Garden of Abdul Gasazi*

Date _____

Dear _____ ,

    Today I am finishing my work on Incredible Stories.  These

stories are alike because _____

_____.

    The strangest thing I read was _____

_____

_____.

    The story I enjoyed most was _____.

I liked the way the author _____

_____.

    If I write a make-believe story, it will be about _____

_____.

Sincerely,

_____

# ALTERNATIVE FORMAT INTEGRATED THEME TESTS

## LEVEL 3.1

## Rewards

# USING THE ALTERNATIVE FORMAT TESTS

## USING AND ADMINISTERING

### Purpose

The Alternative Format Tests provide an opportunity for all students to participate in the evaluation process. By providing summaries of the theme-related text selections and comprehension questions that may be answered orally, each Alternative Format Test enables you to evaluate more accurately the progress of students who may otherwise have difficulty accessing the text selections.

### Description

The Alternative Format Tests include summaries of the authentic reading selections used in the Integrated Theme Tests. Students are asked to respond to the selections by answering comprehension questions. The comprehension questions are in written-response and multiple-choice formats. However, depending on ability level, students may give their answers orally.

### Administering the Alternative Format Tests

Administer the Alternative Format Tests at the same time and in the same manner as you would administer the Integrated Theme Tests. Students taking the Alternative Format Tests should feel that they are participating in the same process as their classmates.

- **Grouping:** The Alternative Format Tests can be administered individually or in a small group. However, if you have several students who may be answering the comprehension questions orally, you may find it easier to evaluate each student if you administer the tests individually.

- **Pacing:** Most students will be able to complete the test in 30–40 minutes. Allow enough time for students to finish the test without rushing.

### Scoring the Test and Modifying Instruction

Answers are provided in the Answer Key on page T21. Score 1 point for each item answered correctly.

If a student scores a 4 or 5 on an Alternative Format Test, continue with extra support and consider using the standard Integrated Theme Test when evaluating the student at the end of the next theme.

If a student consistently scores 3 or below on the Alternative Format Tests, you may want to reconsider your instructional approach or the level of difficulty of the materials the student is using. See also suggestions for further intervention provided on pages T8–T11 of this *Teacher's Edition*.

Name _____

**Read the story summary. Then answer the questions that follow. You may look back at the summary for help.**

# Young Amelia Earhart: A Dream to Fly

**by Susan Alcott**

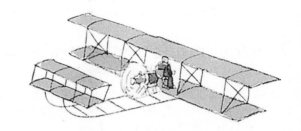

Amelia Earhart was born many years ago. When she was growing up, girls were not allowed to play the same games that boys did.

But Amelia's parents didn't think it was right to treat boys and girls differently. They let Amelia play all kinds of sports.

Amelia grew up and began working as a nurse. The day she saw airplane pilots doing tricks in the air, she made up her mind to learn to fly. After that, Amelia began taking lessons to learn to fly. She practiced flying for a long time. At last, she got her pilot's license.

Amelia became the best woman pilot in the world. She was the first woman to fly across the Atlantic Ocean alone.

After that, Amelia decided to be the first person to fly around the world. A man named Fred Noonan flew with her. They started from Miami, Florida, but something went wrong on the way to Howland Island in the Pacific Ocean. They never arrived there. No one ever heard from Amelia and Fred again.

Amelia Earhart was a very brave woman and what she did still gives people courage today.

1. What made Amelia Earhart decide that she wanted to learn to fly?

   _____

   _____

2. Why might people think Amelia Earhart was a hero?

   _____

   _____

3. As a girl, why did Amelia play games that other girls did not play?

   - ○ **A.** She was stronger than other girls.
   - ○ **B.** Her parents taught her that boys and girls are equal.
   - ○ **C.** She was good at sledding.
   - ○ **D.** She wanted to grow up to be a pilot.

4. Which event happened **after** Amelia got her pilot's license?

   - ○ **F.** She took flying lessons.
   - ○ **G.** She learned to fly at night.
   - ○ **H.** She began working as a nurse.
   - ○ **J.** She flew across the Atlantic Ocean.

5. Which word best describes Amelia Earhart?

   - ○ **A.** scared
   - ○ **B.** good
   - ○ **C.** brave
   - ○ **D.** sad

Name _____

**Read the story summary. Then answer the questions that follow. You may look back at the summary for help.**

# COUNTRY FAIR

**by Gail Gibbons**

The country fair starts today!

Families and friends walk down the midway, the main path through the center of the fairground. There are games to play, foods to eat, and a lot to see. A man yells from a booth, "Test your skills!"

A Ferris wheel slowly turns, taking people high up into the sky. Riders go up and down on the merry-go-round. Everyone loves the rides!

Inside a big building, pumpkins, tomatoes, squash, green beans, and other vegetables are on display. The best fruits and vegetables win blue ribbons.

Over at a fenced-in area, young cows, or calves, are being judged. Other farm animals rest in their stalls, waiting their turn to be judged. Cows and calves moo, while a pig-calling contest is going on. "Sooo-eee!" calls a little boy. Everyone cheers.

At night, a band plays country music. Everyone dances. Fireworks light up the dark sky. *Bang! Pop!* What a good way to end a great day.

1. What can you see and do at a country fair?

_____

_____

2. How does the author show you that fairs are fun?

_____

_____

3. Which of these is a ride you would find at a fair?

   ○ **A.** music
   ○ **B.** Ferris wheel
   ○ **C.** fireworks
   ○ **D.** pig-calling

4. Which detail lets you know that the fair lasts the whole day?

   ○ **F.** At night, a band plays country music.
   ○ **G.** The country fair starts today!
   ○ **H.** Everyone dances.
   ○ **J.** There are games to play, foods to eat, and a lot to see.

5. Why do people bring their animals to the fair?

   ○ **A.** to get the animals checked out by a doctor
   ○ **B.** to let the animals play with each other
   ○ **C.** to give the animals exercise
   ○ **D.** to enter the animals in contests

Name _____

**Read the story summary. Then answer the questions that follow. You can look back at the summary for help.**

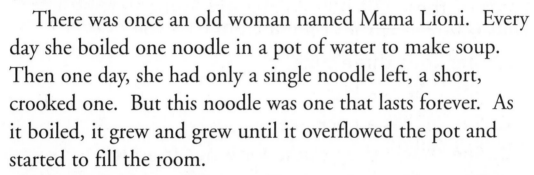

# Mama Lioni's Everlasting Noodle

by Marcia Vaughan

There was once an old woman named Mama Lioni. Every day she boiled one noodle in a pot of water to make soup. Then one day, she had only a single noodle left, a short, crooked one. But this noodle was one that lasts forever. As it boiled, it grew and grew until it overflowed the pot and started to fill the room.

Mama Lioni ate all the noodle soup she could eat. Then she knitted the noodle into three noodle suits. She hung the suits out to dry.

The next morning, three thieves sneaked into her house and took the noodle suits. The thieves planned to tell the villagers that they had been sent to collect taxes. But their real plan was to take the villagers' money and leave town.

And that is what they did — almost. The villagers were fooled and gave the thieves all their money. But before the thieves could run away, it began to rain. It kept raining, and soon the noodle suits got so wet that they fell off the thieves! The villagers knew they had been fooled. They ran after the thieves and caught them.

The villagers gave Mama Lioni a reward. She didn't need anything but the everlasting noodle, so she used the reward to build a home for the orphans of her town.

1. What in this story is make-believe?  Explain your answer.

   _____

   _____

2. Based on the ways she uses the noodle, how would you describe Mama Lioni?

   _____

   _____

3. What is one way that Mama Lioni uses the noodle?

   ○ **A.** She knits three suits.

   ○ **B.** She makes a kite.

   ○ **C.** She makes a necklace.

   ○ **D.** She shares the noodle with her friends.

4. How did the thieves try to fool the villagers?

   ○ **F.** The thieves tried to sell them something that wasn't real.

   ○ **G.** The thieves pretended to be tax collectors.

   ○ **H.** The thieves pretended to be beggars.

   ○ **J.** The thieves pretended to be their friends.

5. How does the story end?

   ○ **A.** The thieves take the money.

   ○ **B.** Mama Lioni makes noodle soup.

   ○ **C.** It rains.

   ○ **D.** Mama Lioni is given a reward.

# ANSWER KEY TO ALTERNATIVE FORMAT TESTS

The answers to the written-response questions are sample answers.
Accept any answers that contain the information provided.

## Theme 1: Off to Adventure!

1. She got excited when she saw pilots doing tricks in the air.
2. She followed her dream and did things no one else had done.
3. B. Her parents taught her that boys and girls are equal.
4. J. She flew across the Atlantic Ocean.
5. C. brave

## Theme 2: Celebrating Traditions

1. You can see animals and people, and you can go on rides and play games.
2. She talks about rides and uses lots of sounds.
3. B. Ferris wheel
4. F. At night, a band plays country music.
5. D. to enter the animals in contests

## Theme 3: Incredible Stories

1. In this story, a noodle that lasts forever and that can be made into clothes is make-believe.
2. She is an old woman who knows how to do many things.
3. A. She knits three suits.
4. G. The thieves pretended to be tax collectors.
5. D. Mama Lioni is given a reward.